The Longevity is Killing Us Series – Book One

LONGEVITY
is
KILLING US

Shallowness Will Bury Us

Richard W. Farwell

RUGGED MAN PUBLISHING

Longevity is Killing Us: Shallowness Will Bury Us

The Longevity is Killing Us Series – Book One

Printed in the United States of America.

Cover image by James Stevens.

Cover design by Lyndsey Barrett, www.AreteDesignStudio.com.

ISBN-10: 0985314907
ISBN-13: 978-0-9853149-0-3

Published by Rugged Man Publishing.
www.ruggedmanpublishing.com.

Dedicated to the dignity and prosperity of the children and grandchildren of seniors worldwide

Table of Contents

Forward... Maybe

In 2008, I wrote an opinion article titled "Longevity is Killing Us," sent to two local papers and the Wall Street Journal. It explained the risk of continuing to promise more entitlements, such as Social Security and Medicare, which were unaffordable even then, and how to solve our growing economic troubles.

By 2011, that risk has multiplied immensely and has also been exposed by our weakened economy. Our elected officials have not been straightforward with us and have been more interested in keeping their jobs and growing their own pensions than in stopping/reversing the downward spiral that our country is on. **We, the "Shallow Electorate," have allowed them to do so.**

Obviously, my first attempt at offering a solution was not successful. It is my deepest desire that this message get out to all who hold the solutions in their own hands, and so I attempt again. While the first time around the article was fully referenced, this exercise is more abbreviated, direct and in the face of the solution holders: *seniors and their loved ones.*

The challenges we Americans and others in the developed world face, namely Europe and Asia, are many. These include weak economic growth, yearly budget deficits, rapidly rising debt levels, costly trade deficits, a weak job and housing market, and overwhelming unfunded entitlement liabilities (i.e., Social Security, Medicare, Medicaid, and private pensions).

While multiple causes apply to each of the above, there is

one thread that runs through them all... high and rising health care costs due to aging populations.

It is the goal of this booklet to confront seniors and their loved ones throughout the world with the expensive truth about end-of-life health costs and to motivate them to make choices that will turn the course of their families and the economy back to strength and prosperity.

If we seniors fail to lead where no one else will tread, then beware when walking the streets alone. If we fail to reverse the current unsustainable redistribution system of wealth from a shrinking and weakened working class to an expanding and demanding retiree class, our children and grandchildren will suffer greatly.

However, if we lead successfully, our economy will grow again, our families will prosper, and America will once again lead the developed and emerging countries on the path to economic and political progress. By getting our act together, we can give hope to the oppressed, many of whom are currently in revolt mode.

Read it, act, and reap – or weep if our shallowness prevails.

Economic Growth

In 2011, economic growth in the USA and throughout the developed world, with a few exceptions, is weak and unbalanced compared to past expansions following recessions. Considering the unprecedented amount of government stimulus thrown at this recovery, our weakness is quite unusual and is due primarily to private industry not releasing their assets because of an anti-business climate.

Our central banker, the Federal Reserve Bank, (aka, the Fed) has also taken an active role in attempting to stimulate our economy by buying $trillions in US Treasuries to keep interest rates and our currency value artificially low. They call it "quantitative easing." While their "easing" may have helped the stock market and kept interest rates low, it hasn't stimulated growth, since banks are still not aggressively lending to small businesses because of the uncertainty about whether consumers will start spending again. Seventy percent of our economy is consumer spending.

Criticism regarding the failed government stimulus is deserved. Criticism for the failed Fed stimulus is not. The Fed knows that tax and regulatory policies from Washington DC are anti-growth. They also know that economic expansion is part of the business cycle, as is peak, contraction, and trough. Typical economic expansion has encouraged inflation in the past. Until it happens this time, the Fed is not worried. They should, however, be worried about government policies muting the business cycle, discouraging the free flow of global capital toward business and ultimately undermining a return to prosperity.

The four principles of capitalism, INCENTIVES to take RISK resulting in SUCCESS or FAILURE, are all being undermined. Why? In a vain pursuit of fairness and to purify human behavior, governments attempt to restrain business from its primary contributions to any society, namely, the primary source of tax revenue, job generation and boundless consumerism. Many in public office do not recognize that human nature can overcome some successful risk takers resulting in excess, greed, corruption, and even arrogance. However, we cannot have success without accepting a certain amount of failure and greed. The price is worth it for our economy and the standard of living we have enjoyed. The price of over-government control is to still have failure and greed, but to also have a lower standard of living.

The Fed also knows that the $trillions in US Treasuries it holds on its books is unprecedented and must ultimately be sold. Since the principle of supply and demand cannot be changed by government edict, the Fed is worried that if the supply of bonds for sale on the open market exceeds demand, bond prices will drop; and since interest rates move inversely with bond prices, interest rate increases would hurt our economic recovery.

Another concern by the Fed is that China and Japan are the largest foreign holders of our debt at approximately $2 trillion. Japan has serious economic problems. Imagine that they need to sell their bonds along with the Fed's obligation to do the same! The rocket rise of interest rates will leave a vapor trail of destruction here and abroad simply because the Fed is receiving little help from our politicians to stimulate growth.

Deficits and Debt – the Underlying Cause

Government budget deficits are also dominant in the news throughout the developed world. These deficits occur when spending on government programs, including interest on debt, is greater than taxes collected. While nearly all elected/appointed officials attempt to close the shortfalls with various painful and often sleight-of-hand strategies, they cannot restrain themselves from the blame game.

The most popular scapegoat in this country accused of causing the great global recession (which began in 2008 resulting in the deficit dilemma) is the real estate bubble and resulting housing market crash from the failure of sub-prime mortgages. (See more detail in Appendix A)

While a few of us small-time advisers warned of a real estate bubble in 2005, some big-time advisers warned the world as well. Yes, we advisers took our advice and made profits by "selling high," but most investors worldwide could not overcome the natural tendencies of greed and complacency.

I reject the argument that the "Great Recession" of 2008 caused the deficits, although it surely reduced taxes collected. While I never like to see human suffering, I'm glad that this event finally exposed the exaggerated entitlement promises that have been made to global citizens since the 1930s. While economic growth/capitalism has lifted millions worldwide out of poverty, it and debt have kept those unfunded promises fully clothed and hidden... at least until recently.

For those who are still unclear about our current and future entitlement promises: THERE IS NO MONEY IN ANY ACCOUNT ANYWHERE SAVED FROM THE MONEY COLLECTED FROM THE TAXPAYERS TO PAY FOR SOCIAL SECURITY AND MEDICARE.

You may wonder, as have I, how such devastating unfunded promises could have been hidden in plain sight for so many decades. Just check the mirror.

Even in this great bastion of freedom and liberty called the USA, we are dominated by what I call the "Shallow Electorate." How else can we explain the actions of the most prosperous of nations falling into the trap of spending all the money for these promised entitlements at the height of economic growth instead of saving the money for the future promises? Yet, that is exactly what we have done. At the height of our economic prowess, we have allowed our elected leaders over the last 50 years to make self-serving and unsustainable financial commitments in the form of so-called entitlements. Many of us have paid a lot into the Social Security fund, only to allow our representatives to spend it all! We have only ourselves to blame for allowing them to do so. We are now suffering the consequences by replacing empty bank accounts with debts that we cannot pay.

It happened to California when the temporary rush of tax revenue from the dot.com bubble during the 1990s led to long-term promises made by those we elected. The burst of the bubble placed its finances in disarray; the state currently verges on bankruptcy. Heck, California is only the eighth largest economy in the world! Again, it is the "Shallow Electorate" of California that allowed their elected leaders to do this. They have only themselves to blame.

Global debt has risen to unsustainable levels as well. While the debt debacles in Greece, Ireland, Spain, Portugal, Italy and even Japan have created much misery for their societies, there is one blessing for sure. They are giving us a glimpse of our future as we continue repeating their errors. Those mistakes include foolish promises, more debt to cover some of the promises, and then refinancing that debt at higher interest rates which lenders require from weakened borrowers. (See Appendix A for more detail)

"The future is our to see..." - Eddie Money

"Compound interest is the most powerful force in the universe." - Albert Einstein

"Debt and revolution are inseparable as cause and effect." - Thomas Jefferson

"Ignore Eddie, Al and Tom at the peril of many." - Yours truly, Rick Farwell

The Tax Code and Regulatory Reform

For decades I have honestly thought I was pretty well informed when it came to this subject of taxes and regulations. My biggest criticism was that since the wealthy pay so much of our tax revenue, why do we have to tax success even more in times of financial crisis?

Now I know why. We have been replacing the limited offspring of the baby boomer generation with low-taxpaying immigrants willing to do the hard labor while baby boomers are now turning 65 at a very fast monthly rate for the next 19 years!

Also, technology-driven globalization has created a permanent unemployment/under-employment situation. While education and training can retool many of our workers, it will take some time, if ever.

The Result: a shrinking middle class leaving the successful as the prime target to pay for our unsustainable promises to the masses and an ever-widening gap between the haves and the have-nots.

It would be great if our representatives followed my favorite president, John F. Kennedy, in reducing tax rates on individuals and business. He made the point very clear, "a rising tide lifts all boats." Of course, reducing tax deductions and simplifying the tax code as well would be necessary. I would happily give up my mortgage deduction if income tax rates dropped as long as the charitable deductions were expanded. Removing government from their self-created role as giver with a catch (vote for me) would be worth it. No longer could they play politics with the most needy.

Whenever a major crisis now occurs, seeking a sound and simple solution is overruled by **blame and regulate**. Regarding the recent "Great Recession," we do not need a multitude of new regulations like Dodd-Frank. We simply need alert and competent regulators armed with stiffer penalties that discourage inappropriate investment behavior.

The same is true regarding the 2002 financial scandals at Enron and World Com resulting in the accounting regulations called Sarbanes-Oxley. These regulations discourage many new companies from going public in this country due to the heavy burden regarding fraud protection and record retention.

Why do we need more regulations regarding altering, destroying, concealing, and cover up? Was fraud legal before? No! Again, all that was necessary was more severe penalties.

Specifically to health care costs, a major contributor is the cost of malpractice insurance. Medical professionals are forced to pay heavily to protect against frivolous and opportunistic lawsuits, be they individual or class action. Tort reform is overdue and continually ignored. Trial lawyers are thrilled. Be it taxation or all of the other numerous regulations placed upon us by our elected officials, there seems to be a lack of concern by the Shallow Electorate. Bureaucracies are such a growth industry here in this country that nearly twice as many work for the government than in manufacturing. Our job killers are getting away with murder.

The exposé has begun. Does anyone care?

What about Budget Cuts?

Budget cuts at the margin are the *austere du jour* for most global politicians and in this country for sure. They will threaten to cut Social Security and Medicare, or police, fire, education, and military, *but then* cut from the non-voters (the poor, the young, the infirm and the needy) *and seldom* cut from seniors (the largest voting block) even though the main threat to our prosperity is the promises to seniors which are inherently broken. The non-voters contribute little to political action committees. Better that than true reform at the heart of the problem... health care and retirement?

Unfunded entitlement promises are now exposed, as economic weakness continues and as the ranks of seniors expand. We are a serious constituency. Hands off our Social Security and Medicare! The politicians choose to sacrifice the future of younger Americans rather than lose the votes of the seniors.

How does the Shallow Electorate respond to salt on the open wounds of America? No complaint unless the blood is on their carpet, as in losing their own jobs.

Granted, we have had some aggressive demonstrations by college students in California and union supporters in Wisconsin and Minnesota. Nothing, however, like the young French rioting in the streets of Paris in October 2010 opposing a retirement age change from 60 to 62! God forbid. Perhaps Americans have been calm because many so-called cuts have just been sleight-of-hand movement of funds from one account to another or from one time frame to another. Some of our budget manipulators are masters at this. I wonder if one can obtain a PhD in budget baloney? When real cuts do occur, I'll bet our streets will be full of rioters, too!

Voting Power... an Oxymoron?

If you are looking to this chapter on voting power for answers to the multitude of questions presented to this point, forget it.

The reason I am so critical of our Shallow Electorate is simply because there is so much evidence in our face each day. Have you noticed that looks, body language, oratory skills, and repetitive sound bites of politicians resonate with so many voters over their actual messages and actions?

Have you noticed that we are facing multiple challenges in our country and abroad? Social Security, Medicare, Medicaid, debt, deficits, government employee pensions, and unfunded liabilities are the biggies. The current budget and debt debate in Washington, DC, and most state capitals is intense.

We elected these representatives to make the easy *and* tough choices, which is our form of government. So why do they avoid making the changes needed?

Imagine winning an election with 52% of the votes cast. Say, for example, that the election turnout was 50% of registered voters. Now imagine that the unregistered citizens in the jurisdiction, including children, represent 50% of total residents. After donning your math cap, you will confirm that only 13% of all residents to be represented by the winner actually voted for the winner! Now, which of the constituents do you believe the winner will listen to during the term and especially as the next campaign for reelection heats up? I believe that leaves 87%

out in the cold.

Seriously, how long do you believe we can keep up this charade parade of vote accumulation when we need action to secure the present and the future?

Obamacare passed by strict party lines. It required that under a centralized health care plan, government must make cost judgments on all treatments and drugs as to what is best for society. When the cost judgment law was criticized as a death panel, it was changed to a regulation called "comparative effectiveness research." Either way, a committee will decide what is covered and what isn't.

The recent Republican plan for health care recommends we privatize Medicare and push Medicaid responsibilities to the states. Dead on arrival for sure. Let's assume, though, that this Medicare plan was adopted. It would not apply to those citizens over 55 *or* now on the current program. Certainly wouldn't want to upset any voting seniors with action now!

Either way, the federal government, state governments, or insurance companies will decide which kind of benefits we will receive at the end of our life. Which one do you like? Even though our leaders get paid good salaries, free health care, and a generous pension based upon their reelection (they receive more money in their pension the longer that they serve), most of them make an appearance of fixing it, but actually just defer the problems to the next group of politicians. I have a better way... hang in there. Your vote is not dead yet!

Entitlements are NOT "Free"!!!

The depression of the 1930s ended when late in the decade President Roosevelt reversed some anti-business policies and World War II began. After the war, pensions were offered to both public and private workers. Social Security was also introduced with the eligibility age beyond average life expectancy. No problem there... then.

The Baby Boomers were born between 1946 and 1964, so there were plenty of young, hard-working families helping to build America's economy with plenty of time before retirement.

It wasn't until the 1970s when our government concluded that private pensions were underfunded. They required businesses to apply more of their profits to the private pension shortfalls instead of dividends to stockholders, bonuses to executives and staff, or business expansion. Since the bottom line is key to business success, many owners exercised the "free" in free market capitalism and moved from defined benefits plans (pensions) to defined contribution plans (401(k)s). This required employees to help fund their retirement by choosing an investment strategy and an appropriate level of risk.

I am a fan of private industry and describe it as the goose that lays plenty of golden eggs at the feet of government. While imperfect, business success truly helps provide the revenue to support the many services and social programs from which we all benefit.

Unfortunately, when private pensions were forced to change due to underfunding, that was not the case with public pensions or Social Security. Even when money earned was short of the funds' requirements, the public shortfalls were ignored by the politicians and simply added to the unfunded liability.

Well, here we are today. Unfunded liabilities (the money the government has promised and supposedly collected for health care and retirement but that has been spent for other unrelated government programs) are now estimated to be in excess of $100 trillion and growing. What was good for the goose (business forced to address a serious issue) didn't apply to the gander (public officials ignoring a serious issue).

Longevity is Killing Us

Even if no action is taken on Social Security and public pension reform, these two issues are like ice compared to the red hot issue of health care.

Health care statistics are overwhelming and scary and just too many to detail. Here is just a sample. For more, just pick up any newspaper, magazine, turn on a television business show or search the web.

- Health care costs are the fastest growing part of our federal budget and the most serious and sensitive to deal with.
- While the vast majority of Americans do not want cuts in their health care and Social Security benefits, over the next ten years our spending is projected to rise by 71% for Social Security, 72% for Medicare and 115% for Medicaid.
- 28% of Medicare expenses occur in the last year of life.
- In 2008, 1% of Medicaid beneficiaries represented 25% of total Medicaid costs.
- Seniors who retired in 2010 will spend during the rest of their life expectancy THREE TIMES the amount of premiums they paid in.

UNHEALTHY longevity is killing us. It's killing our economy, and it's killing our individual dignity.

As entitlement costs overwhelm federal and state budgets, globalization, weak economic growth, and retiring baby boomers will stress those budgets even more. Medical research funded by the National Institute of Health (NIH) reveals that we are experiencing a lethal-to-chronic disease transition. If patients survive lethal disease, they then deal with chronic disease, treatment, and pain. As Baby Boomers retire, it means a greater fraction of elders are now on the planet than ever in the history of mankind! While boomers work and play hard, they are healthy enough to survive many early lethal health issues only to face the multitude of chronic diseases that can make later aging miserable and really expensive. Also, as they battle old age, they will face an aging medical profession as experienced general practitioners retire and many young and bright medical students seek high-paying specialty careers. This will make it more difficult to even get an initial appointment with a doctor. Better keep exercising and dieting!

Now for a global perspective on health care: a report published in Bloomberg Businessweek, Feb 28, 2011, reveals that of the thirty developed countries measured in 2007, America's life expectancy is shorter than all but SIX, while our cost per person is the MOST EXPENSIVE by far ($7,290 per person compared to the average of $2,954 for the other twenty-nine countries!).

What do you think? Do we have plenty of time for our leaders to consider more options and contingencies and call for more meetings and commissions?

Perhaps expanding government, more centralization, more control over private commerce, breaking the link between taxation and representation, making things fairer, health care for all, carbon tax and reluctance to deploy the military is the correct way. No, that is not me talking about the USA. I am just repeating a warning from Daniel Hannan, a member of the European Parliament, who is British and thinks we are making the same mistakes Great Britain made.

Mr. Hannan is brave to be so direct and reminds me of the old saying, "Experience is not the best teacher. Better to learn from the experience of others."

Will we learn, or just continue piling on more debt for our children with budget shortfalls, trade deficits, and greater unfunded liabilities?

Recent polls indicate the American public (regardless of political leaning) does not want any substantial changes to Medicare/Medicaid and favors taxing the rich and successful to cover budget shortfalls. Those two public positions are death-anxiety driven and ignore the truth. The painful truth is high employment costs, rising budget/trade deficits and debt are driven in large part by rising health care costs sending many multinational companies overseas. The small businesses that are strictly domestic are usually run by those successful business owners the public wants to tax more, undermining those businesses before they've been taxed. While the public does not favor raising the debt ceiling, they do not want to address rising employment costs while expecting higher taxes to stimulate job and economic growth!

Also, while the majority of seniors want to spend their last days at home, a report on "60 Minutes" revealed that 75% of seniors die in a hospital or nursing home thus greatly increasing the costs of Medicare.

If we don't fix the system soon, then riots, crime, and the worst that is possible in a societal breakdown will be our current and future reality.

Perhaps my definition of the public as "the Shallow Electorate" is far too nice.

You have just one guess who will pay the bill in the future. You may have even brought a few of them into this world. Their numbers and their positive attitude will be shrinking as they work off the debts and have to cover the growing ranks of the aged while bearing a great tax burden. They are our children, and they deserve much more from us than our shallow, selfish fearfulness.

Our shallowness will bury us... and it will bury them.

In Summary

One of my favorite oxymorons, *conventional wisdom*, suggests America and other developed nations (another of the favorites) blend together some growth stimulation with a splash of cost cutting, a dash of regulatory fine-tuning, a big scoop of tax increases on the successful and finally mix in many cups of additional borrowing. Once heated, this combination (however measured) will rise to "engulp" us all. Unwise and poorly developed thinking, for sure.

For those who do not spend much time in the kitchen, let me by more succinct. Under our current economic and political systems as they have both evolved and eroded, we can no longer expect our elected officials to grow, borrow, tax, spend, cut, or regulate our way back to prosperity.

While these actions may have worked in the past, they don't any more. We are too far down the wrong recipe. no longer can we have our cake and treat it with such disregard. Now the cake is so big that even if they cut regulation and taxes to allow business to grow and capitalism to do its work, it's too little too late. The debt and liabilities are way too large. We cannot wait for politicians to fix this. Somebody has to start paying for all of the promises to the expanding elderly, and it cannot be solely the shrinking young. Even David Brooks, columnist for the New York Times, agrees that we must reverse our redistribution system.

I say it must start now.

Numerous issues have been brought to these pages. Just like many of you, I have been deluged by them all. Each of them has its own set of multiple solutions making the answers even more elusive and conflicting.

Is it any wonder that no one seems to have a simple solution to them all? I sure didn't until three years ago when my first attempt at explanation fell upon deaf ears. Since then, I have watched the global recession increase the misery of many. Some have even taken their frustrations to the streets. The catalyst for my concern was an article by Francis Fukuyama regarding human dignity. Here is the quote: "All social revolutions are driven by intense anger over injured dignity, often crystallized by a single event or image."

I was not charged by the dignity seekers of the Middle East as much as the loss of dignity by so many in Europe, Japan and Mexico and by what our future generations will suffer as we set them up for failure.

America, until recently, has been a role model for the world as well as a defender and buyer of last resort. If we can correct our problems soon, we can lead Europe and Japan and others in the industrialized world out of their mess. We can also give guidance to the emerging countries on what to avoid. Finally, a strengthened America could be a powerful example for rebels and rebels-to-be that liberty/freedom is not easy but possible and worth the effort if one is willing to earn it.

If we want to recapture our position as the leader of the free world, we must recognize one alarming truth: we will only be able to grow our economy, reduce our budget and trade deficits, reduce our debt and unfunded liabilities and improve our job prospects at home (which will revive our housing market) *by substantially reducing our health care costs.*

The "we" I am referring to is not our elected officials. I hope I have made that perfectly clear! The "we" I am referring to are *<u>all seniors</u> across this great country and around the globe.*

Dear Seniors,

Can't you **see** what debt, government dependence and unkept promises have done to Europe, Japan and the US?

Can't you **hear** the complaints from the unemployed and the underemployed questioning how they can provide for their family and retirement?

Can't you **feel** for those in real need who are taking the first and easy hits from budget cuts?

Can't you **understand** that something has to change soon to fix the future and not put it off for another decade or more?

Can't you **acknowledge** that most politicians lack the courage to act and compromise on major issues if it means losing votes?

Can't you **sense** that just maybe you do have some power to solve big problems?

How can you say that you love your country, but instead reject President John F. Kennedy's challenge? "Ask not what your country can do for you, but what you can do for your country."

How can you say you love your children and grandchildren but are willing to add hundreds of thousands of dollars to a mountain of unfunded entitlement promises that could destroy their health, their family finances and especially their dignity?

We seniors, without the help of others (and in spite of human nature), can decide to not spend all of that money in the last year of life. In doing so, we can change just about everything I have highlighted in this booklet which ultimately seeks the dignity of every person, young and old.

We seniors must attempt and encourage others to live lives which are long and **healthy** but to not prolong lives which are **unhealthy**.

How can you say you believe in a God or even fate but will not take the call when it's your time? Instead, you allow a doctor or loved one to answer. Why are you so afraid of death, so afraid to meet your maker? Is it that you don't really believe how beautiful heaven is... or perhaps you just are not a true believer?

The Solution:
ACTIONS – Not Reaction, Inaction or Delay

STEP ONE – We seniors must emphasize and improve our health first by good old-fashioned diet and exercise. However, once our health fails, then it is critical that we limit end-of-life costs by saying NO and having step two in place. If you are a senior covered by Medicare, ask the doctor who is recommending expensive treatment/drugs what the total cost will be to that government program including follow up treatment. If it is more than you have paid in Medicare premiums, say no. If yes, you are just adding to an estimated $100 trillion in unfunded entitlement liabilities your offspring will succumb under. Place your loved ones well ahead of human nature.

STEP TWO – We seniors must immediately begin end-of-life planning by preparing an advanced directive, revealing our clear intentions if we are incapacitated using:

- A Living Will
- A Medical Power of Attorney
- Five Wishes
- POLST (Physician Orders for Life Sustaining Treatment)

I recommend POLST, as it is prepared in conjunction with your doctor. It is recorded and cannot be lost when it is needed and requires no medical power of attorney. See a copy at the end of this booklet, and find it online at www.polst.org.

Mine reads:

A) CPR – Allow natural death

B) Medical interventions – comfort measures only

C) Artificially administered nutrition – no artificial nutrition by tube

STEP THREE – We seniors and other voters must find a leader(s) (political or not) that will promote the concept of a SINGLE TERM POLITICAL SYSTEM.

I favor four years for the House of Representatives, eight years for the Senate, and six years for the Presidency... with easier recall procedures.

We are trapped in a scenario where bold actions by elected officials is not taken due to their *re-election conflict of interest*. (Remember, not only do they avoid tough decisions in order to be re-elected, but the longer they serve, the larger their pension.) Also, they typically spend and promise more in good times resulting in even more pain when the economy weakens (like now).

A system of longer, single terms is needed with a good salary and health care provided. Once their term is up, the ex-politician pays for health care individually. The pension should be a defined contribution plan (401(k)), not a defined benefit plan (a traditional pension). Career politicians are undermining our future, and we cannot allow them to spend what our actions will save. A simpler political system, as was originally designed, will allow the elected to then make the important economic decisions that the current multi-term system undermines. Just imagine, they will actually be working full-time for us!

STEP FOUR – As an incentive for some seniors who may hesitate at making these difficult choices that will make a difference here at home and throughout the developed world, I propose that Congress provide a death benefit payment to beneficiaries of seniors on Medicare/Medicaid which would be reduced by health care expenses incurred during the last year of life. For example, if the government provides $100,000 in death benefit, but a senior receives $25,000 in health care from the government in the last year of life, then the death benefit payment for loved ones would be $75,000. However, if the senior receives $100,000 in health care from the government in the last year, then the death benefit payment for loved ones would be $0.

Note: We seniors must take the lead. Steps 1 and 2 have to be done first and are mutually exclusive of 3 and 4. Step 3 should naturally follow 1 and 2. Step 4 is my attempt to again change your human nature to make choices in the best interest of your offspring over yourself.

Conclusion

Let me be clear about the big picture. America is not off track. Derailment always ends in serious crumple. We are simply off course. We seniors must now take the lead by reversing the redistribution system. We must begin giving back to our country and to future generations.

Once we do begin, leaders will emerge who can correct our weakened political and economic systems. They will only accomplish that great feat by reaching past shallowness to the depths of the American spirit.

One final quote by, you guessed it, my favorite president, JFK. While this was presented to the General Assembly of the United Nations in 1961 in reference to terrorism, it applies to us seniors today. "Americans are not afraid to die for a life worth living." In contrast, today many are afraid to die for a life *not* worth living. I believe that, together, we seniors can not only solve the world's problems, but save our loved ones from the serious terror of poverty, riots, crime and the worst that is possible in a societal breakdown.

Even if some of JFK's principles are ignored or rejected, how can we reject the brave sacrifices of heroes past fighting for our freedom and independence by seeking dependence? How can we be so disrespectful of our military and law enforcement?

Yes, this booklet is controversial. No, it is not meant to be political. If anything, it's anti-political and anti-human nature. What are the chances of global success in my lifetime? That's up to you. What are the chances of me giving up? NEVER!!!

Remember, unhealthy longevity is killing us, and our shallowness will bury us.

Epilogue

October 23, 2011

Upon completion of this booklet in mid-2011, I certainly didn't expect my only sibling, a younger brother, to bring the issue of longevity of life so close to home.

While the oncologist has declared my brother terminal with debilitating bone cancer, one member of the immediate family will not accept the diagnosis and wants further tests and procedures. If insurance will not cover additional costs, I have been asked to provide financial assistance.

My answer is yes, since any support I offer is my choice and mortgages no one's future.

Appendix A: Debts & Deficits – Details

The most popular scapegoats in this country are those accused of causing the great global recession which began in 2008 resulting in the deficit dilemma:

- Congress encouraged banks to make home loans to unqualified borrowers seeking "The American Dream."
- Congress then encouraged government agencies to purchase those loans freeing the lenders to continue the process for more profit.
- Wall Street then packaged those loans in complicated style for sale across the globe for even more profit.
- Rating agencies that were coerced by Congress into giving AAA ratings to these newly called "sub-prime" loan packages.
- US regulators were sometimes asleep, often ignored and, at times, even cooperative in the process.
- Global purchasers of those loan packages ignored customary due diligence and committed the most basic of investing sins by "buying high."

Debt

Just a few words about global debt. It cannot provide cover any longer for spendthrift economies now that it has been exposed as another easy way out that mortgages the future.

Global debt is best measured as a percentage of a country's economic output (i.e., gross domestic product/GDP/total of goods produced and services offered). Imagine you own a business that produces $100,000 from sales of a widget. Expenses total $50,000. Your profit before taxes is $50,000. If sales drop to $75,000 and you cannot cut expenses, your profit drops to $25,000. If you decide to borrow $25,000 to maintain living costs, your debt is 33% of your economic output.

While our debt hit a high of 150% of GDP following World War II, we are now near 100% and could handle more if economic growth is expected to be strong. Doubtful for sure, leaving our polarized politicians with many poor choices... the worst being more debt or inflation.

A number of European countries and Japan have debt levels at historic highs with no guarantees they can survive another crisis, man-made or natural! Japan is especially exposed. It not only is hurting from its recent natural disaster, but has not experienced strong economic growth for decades. Its aging population will experience the largest wave of baby-boomers retiring in 2012. How will a smaller working class in these indebted nations be able to pay down the debt and the interest compounding on that debt if growth is weak? How can we?

Trade Deficits

Everyone I know would trade deficits for surplus, but playing with words doesn't solve problems. That is unless one is a politician seeking reelection and a larger pension.

Trade deficits refer to a country's foreign purchases (imports) in excess of their shipments to foreign buyers (exports).

Our country has a substantial trade deficit. The last time I can recall a trade surplus was just recently in California. Sorry, no trend here. What just happened is a confluence of unique events: artificially low interest rates keeping our dollar weak while helping exports, a weak economy resulting in our reduced consumption plus higher energy and food prices, driving up the costs of imports.

No worry. Soon we will be back to higher interest rates, normal energy and food costs, and hopefully, an economy with moderate growth resulting in more trade deficits. This scenario has exposed our high structural cost of goods and services produced in this country, which has driven our trade deficits for decades.

All but two of our states have more employees in government than in private manufacturing. In fact, the country has nearly twice as many public employees as private workers who actually make things. Alas, we have a growing trade deficit, as we have priced ourselves out of much of the export market but keep buying cheap imports.

As our employment costs have risen, "free" enterprise/capitalism/businesses (however you want to define the private sector) simply moved some employment offshore where labor is cheaper. They still have a profit motive, unlike most politicians.

Do not assume that the bad guys here are simply the American companies that participate in the global trade community. Our domestic employers also include self-employed entrepreneurs, domestic-only companies, and all government entities. Be assured that all employers in this country take advantage of cheap foreign labor. Some use foreign operators and customer service employees for their toll-free lines, and all probably use foreign parts and/or materials of some kind. It is unlikely you will find one government desk drawer full of only "made in America" items.

While criticizing greedy corporations for being so un-American by hiring cheap foreign labor, our elected leaders then cleverly replace those lost manufacturing jobs with public workers using promises galore while borrowing from foreign investors to cover the shortfall.

Whatever few manufacturing jobs we have left, they represent our innovation and uniqueness, which overcome the high cost of taxes, regulations, and entitlements in the global trade environment. Apple, Google, Facebook and Caterpillar come to mind.

With technology-led globalization and the ever challenging rise in labor costs, it is unlikely we can bring about a more balanced trade picture soon. There is some hope, though, as presented in the Solution chapter of this booklet.

Appendix B: P.O.L.S.T.

HIPAA PERMITS DISCLOSURE OF POLST TO OTHER HEALTH CARE PROVIDERS AS NECESSARY

Physician Orders for Life-Sustaining Treatment (POLST)

EMSA #111 B
(Effective 4/1/2011)

First follow these orders, then contact physician. This is a Physician Order Sheet based on the person's current medical condition and wishes. Any section not completed implies full treatment for that section. A copy of the signed POLST form is legal and valid. POLST complements an Advance Directive and is not intended to replace that document. Everyone shall be treated with dignity and respect.

Patient Last Name:	Date Form Prepared:
Patient First Name:	Patient Date of Birth:
Patient Middle Name:	Medical Record #: *(optional)*

A *Check One*

CARDIOPULMONARY RESUSCITATION (CPR): ***If person has no pulse and is not breathing. When NOT in cardiopulmonary arrest, follow orders in Sections B and C.***

- ☐ **Attempt Resuscitation/CPR** (Selecting CPR in Section A **requires** selecting Full Treatment in Section B)
- ☐ **Do Not Attempt Resuscitation/DNR** (Allow Natural Death)

B *Check One*

MEDICAL INTERVENTIONS: ***If person has pulse and/or is breathing.***

- ☐ **Comfort Measures Only** Relieve pain and suffering through the use of medication by any route, positioning, wound care and other measures. Use oxygen, suction and manual treatment of airway obstruction as needed for comfort. ***Transfer to hospital only*** *if comfort needs cannot be met in current location.*
- ☐ **Limited Additional Interventions** In addition to care described in Comfort Measures Only, use medical treatment, antibiotics, and IV fluids as indicated. Do not intubate. May use non-invasive positive airway pressure. Generally avoid intensive care.
  - ☐ ***Transfer to hospital only*** *if comfort needs cannot be met in current location.*
- ☐ **Full Treatment** In addition to care described in Comfort Measures Only and Limited Additional Interventions, use intubation, advanced airway interventions, mechanical ventilation, and defibrillation/cardioversion as indicated. ***Transfer to hospital*** *if indicated. Includes intensive care.*

Additional Orders: ______________________________

C *Check One*

ARTIFICIALLY ADMINISTERED NUTRITION: ***Offer food by mouth if feasible and desired.***

- ☐ No artificial means of nutrition, including feeding tubes.
- ☐ Trial period of artificial nutrition, including feeding tubes.
- ☐ Long-term artificial nutrition, including feeding tubes.

Additional Orders: ______________________________

D

INFORMATION AND SIGNATURES:

Discussed with: ☐ Patient (Patient Has Capacity) ☐ Legally Recognized Decisionmaker

- ☐ Advance Directive dated _______ available and reviewed →
- ☐ Advance Directive not available
- ☐ No Advance Directive

Health Care Agent if named in Advance Directive:
Name: ______________________
Phone: ______________________

Signature of Physician

My signature below indicates to the best of my knowledge that these orders are consistent with the person's medical condition and preferences.

Print Physician Name:	Physician Phone Number:	Physician License Number:
Physician Signature: *(required)*		Date:

Signature of Patient or Legally Recognized Decisionmaker

By signing this form, the legally recognized decisionmaker acknowledges that this request regarding resuscitative measures is consistent with the known desires of, and with the best interest of, the individual who is the subject of the form.

Print Name:		Relationship: *(write self if patient)*
Signature: *(required)*		Date:
Address:	Daytime Phone Number:	Evening Phone Number:

SEND FORM WITH PERSON WHENEVER TRANSFERRED OR DISCHARGED

HIPAA PERMITS DISCLOSURE OF POLST TO OTHER HEALTH CARE PROVIDERS AS NECESSARY

Patient Information

Name (last, first, middle):	Date of Birth:	Gender: **M F**

Health Care Provider Assisting with Form Preparation

Name:	Title:	Phone Number:

Additional Contact

Name:	Relationship to Patient:	Phone Number:

Directions for Health Care Provider

Completing POLST

- Completing a POLST form is voluntary. California law requires that a POLST form be followed by health care providers, and provides immunity to those who comply in good faith. In the hospital setting, a patient will be assessed by a physician who will issue appropriate orders.
- POLST does not replace the Advance Directive. When available, review the Advance Directive and POLST form to ensure consistency, and update forms appropriately to resolve any conflicts.
- POLST must be completed by a health care provider based on patient preferences and medical indications.
- A legally recognized decisionmaker may include a court-appointed conservator or guardian, agent designated in an Advance Directive, orally designated surrogate, spouse, registered domestic partner, parent of a minor, closest available relative, or person whom the patient's physician believes best knows what is in the patient's best interest and will make decisions in accordance with the patient's expressed wishes and values to the extent known.
- POLST must be signed by a physician and the patient or decisionmaker to be valid. Verbal orders are acceptable with follow-up signature by physician in accordance with facility/community policy.
- Certain medical conditions or treatments may prohibit a person from residing in a residential care facility for the elderly.
- If a translated form is used with patient or decisionmaker, attach it to the signed English POLST form.
- Use of original form is strongly encouraged. Photocopies and FAXes of signed POLST forms are legal and valid. A copy should be retained in patient's medical record, on Ultra Pink paper when possible.

Using POLST

- Any incomplete section of POLST implies full treatment for that section.

Section A:

- If found pulseless and not breathing, no defibrillator (including automated external defibrillators) or chest compressions should be used on a person who has chosen "Do Not Attempt Resuscitation."

Section B:

- When comfort cannot be achieved in the current setting, the person, including someone with "Comfort Measures Only," should be transferred to a setting able to provide comfort (e.g., treatment of a hip fracture).
- Non-invasive positive airway pressure includes continuous positive airway pressure (CPAP), bi-level positive airway pressure (BiPAP), and bag valve mask (BVM) assisted respirations.
- IV antibiotics and hydration generally are not "Comfort Measures."
- Treatment of dehydration prolongs life. If person desires IV fluids, indicate "Limited Interventions" or "Full Treatment."
- Depending on local EMS protocol, "Additional Orders" written in Section B may not be implemented by EMS personnel.

Reviewing POLST

It is recommended that POLST be reviewed periodically. Review is recommended when:

- The person is transferred from one care setting or care level to another, or
- There is a substantial change in the person's health status, or
- The person's treatment preferences change.

Modifying and Voiding POLST

- A patient with capacity can, at any time, request alternative treatment.
- A patient with capacity can, at any time, revoke a POLST by any means that indicates intent to revoke. It is recommended that revocation be documented by drawing a line through Sections A through D, writing "VOID" in large letters, and signing and dating this line.
- A legally recognized decisionmaker may request to modify the orders, in collaboration with the physician, based on the known desires of the individual or, if unknown, the individual's best interests.

This form is approved by the California Emergency Medical Services Authority in cooperation with the statewide POLST Task Force. For more information or a copy of the form, visit **www.caPOLST.org**.

SEND FORM WITH PERSON WHENEVER TRANSFERRED OR DISCHARGED

About the Author

Rick Farwell is married with two children and nine grandchildren. He is financially secure, having no pension other than Social Security. He and his wife, Darlene, worked hard, lived conservatively, and saved regularly to now enjoy a comfortable retirement (thank you 401(k)!).

In his early twenties after college, Rick enlisted in the US. Navy, serving as a radar operator on a Grumman S2-A (anti-submarine aircraft). He was a sailor but never on a ship. It was thrilling to have the squadron commander as his pilot!

During his nearly fifty-year career in the financial services industry, he attained the level of head office manager in the Savings and Loan industry, worked his way up to CEO of a nationally renowned credit union, and eventually owned his own financial planning business advising clients in maintaining and increasing their wealth through two tumultuous decades.

Before retiring, Rick was a Certified Financial Planner, a Certified Fund Specialist, a Certified Retirement Counselor, a licensed insurance agent and a stockbroker.

His passion grows daily as he attempts to help the world understand that the answer to solving current economic challenges lies not with government but with individuals currently unwilling to make the tough choices for the welfare of their children and grandchildren.

You can follow Rick on his blog: www.rickfarwell.com.

Made in United States
North Haven, CT
04 November 2026

21770183R00029